making gingerbread houses
and other gingerbread treats

Joanna Farrow
Photographs by Michelle Garrett

This edition is published by Southwater

Southwater is an imprint of
Anness Publishing Limited
Hermes House
88–89 Blackfriars Road
London SE1 8HA
tel. 020 7401 2077
fax 020 7633 9499

Distributed in the UK by
The Manning Partnership
251–253 London Road East
Batheaston
Bath BA1 7RL
tel. 01225 852 727
fax 01225 852 852

Distributed in the USA by
Anness Publishing Inc.
27 West 20th Street
Suite 504
New York
NY 10011
tel. 212 807 6739
fax 212 807 6813

Distributed in Australia by
Sandstone Publishing
Unit 1
360 Norton Street
Leichhardt
New South Wales 2040
tel. 02 9560 7888
fax 02 9560 7488

3 5 7 9 10 8 6 4 2

Publisher: Joanna Lorenz
Editorial Manager: Helen Sudell
Designer: Bobbie Colgate Stone
Photographer and Stylist: Michelle Garrett
Home Economist: Joanna Farrow, assisted by Julie Beresford
Illustrator: Lucinda Ganderton

Templates
Some of the templates at the back of the book will need scaling up to the required size. If you have access to a photocopier
it will do the job for you. Otherwise, copy the template on to tracing paper, draw a squared grid over it, and transfer the template, square by square, on to a
sheet of larger scale graph paper.

Previously published as Gingerbread

CONTENTS

INTRODUCTION

ONE OF THE MOST ANCIENT of spices, ginger has been traded across the world for centuries, resulting in a wonderful array of uses, especially as a flavoring for sweet cakes and cookies. Ornately decorated, festive houses, spiced fruit cakes, yeasted sweet loaves and tea breads, chunky cookies and moist, sticky cakes, can all be accurately described as "gingerbread."

All the different types of ginger available come from fresh ginger, a fibrous, woody root that can be used freshly grated in both sweet and savory dishes. In gingerbread, it is usually the dried and ground root, sold as a powder, that gives the spicy flavor. Stem, crystallized and candied ginger and all forms of preserved young ginger can also be chopped and added to ginger cakes, cookies, breads, fillings and icings.

This book demonstrates the decorative value of baking gingerbread. Gingerbread has become increasingly popular over the last century but has been around for hundreds of years. In medieval Europe, when fairs were widely enjoyed, gingerbread was sold in pretty shapes, often gilded and studded with spices. Fairs became known as "Gingerbread Fairs" and fairgoers would buy gingerbread for gifts, or "fairings."

♥ *Sturdy metal cutters are perfect for shaping gingerbread hearts.*

Nuremberg, in Germany, became known as the "Gingerbread Capital of the World," because of its central position on the northern trade routes. Here, the art of making gingerbread molds to shape ornate gingerbread carvings was developed. They were made into the shapes of kings and queens, windmills, letters, hearts and animals. When baked and decorated, these elaborate shapes were frequently gilded with gold paint and sold at markets and fairs.

The German fairy tale Hansel and Gretel, in which the children discover a house made entirely of gingerbread, candy and cake, inspired the trend for making beautiful constructions based on gingerbread. These often have a "fairy tale" appearance, dusted with confectioners' sugar and traditionally presented to friends at Christmas.

Today, most people associate gingerbread with Christmas, but there are many other times of year when it makes a delicious gift or simply a creative treat for the whole family. A cleverly constructed castle, train or cottage makes an impressive birthday cake for children and the young at heart. Decorative gingerbread cookies also make lovely gifts, wrapped in tissue and beautifully presented in an ornate box or tin with ribbon decoration.

WORKING WITH GINGERBREAD

There are several points to remember when working with gingerbread for the first time. You might find it easier to shape large, cutout pieces of gingerbread on the cookie sheet, so that the dough doesn't distort as you transfer it from the work surface. Unless the recipe instructs otherwise, space the pieces slightly apart on the cookie sheet, to allow room for expansion.

Like any cookie, gingerbread is not crisp or firm when it first comes out of the oven; this means it can be difficult to tell whether it is done, particularly as baking times vary from oven to oven. Generally, the cookies will have risen slightly and will just be coloring around the edges. Leave the gingerbread on the cookie sheet for a few minutes, in which time it will start to crisp. (If the gingerbread still feels very soft, return it to the oven for a few minutes.) Often, the gingerbread will distort slightly during baking, but you can easily trim it afterward.

Large, flat pieces of gingerbread must be cooled and stored on a flat surface or they will become distorted. For convenience, you may prefer to make the gingerbread a day before decorating it. If so, let it cool completely and then wrap it in waxed paper or cover it with plastic wrap.

♥ *These gingerbread cookies were made using an assortment of cutters and decorated with ribbon and piped icing.*

BASIC RECIPES AND TECHNIQUES

B oth Golden Gingerbread and Chocolate Gingerbread are frequently used in this book for shaping into buildings and other constructions, as they can be thinly rolled and have a firm texture. Lebkuchen has a slightly softer texture, perfect for little and shaped cookies. If using the dough for a recipe project, wrap and chill the gingerbread, and then refer to the project for the shaping method. Alternatively, make simple cookies by cutting out shapes with a cutter and baking them at 350°F for about 12 minutes, until they are just beginning to color around the edges.

GOLDEN GINGERBREAD

1¼ cups all-purpose flour
¼ teaspoon baking soda
pinch of salt
1 teaspoon ground ginger
1 teaspoon ground cinnamon
5 tablespoons sweet butter,
cut into pieces
½ cup superfine sugar
2 tablespoons maple syrup
1 egg yolk, beaten

1 Sift together the flour, baking soda, salt and spices. Rub the butter into the flour in a large bowl, until the mixture resembles fine bread crumbs. Alternatively, blend in a food processor.

2 Add the sugar, syrup and egg yolk and mix or process to a firm dough. Knead lightly. Wrap and chill for 30 minutes before shaping.

CHOCOLATE GINGERBREAD

1¼ cups all-purpose flour
pinch of salt
2 teaspoons ground pumpkin-pie spice
½ teaspoon baking soda
¼ cup cocoa powder
6 tablespoons sweet butter,
cut into pieces
½ cup brown sugar
1 egg, beaten

1 Sift together the flour, salt, spice, baking soda and cocoa powder. Blend in a food processor, with the butter, until the mixture resembles fine bread crumbs. Alternatively, knead the butter into the flour in a large bowl.

2 Add the sugar and egg and mix to a firm dough. Knead lightly. Wrap in plastic wrap and chill for at least 30 minutes before shaping.

LEBKUCHEN

*8 tablespoons (1 stick) sweet
butter, softened
¼ cup brown sugar
1 egg, beaten
1 cup molasses
3 cups self-rising flour
1 teaspoon ground ginger
½ teaspoon ground cloves
¼ teaspoon chili powder*

1 Cream together the butter and sugar until pale and fluffy. Beat in the egg and molasses. Sift the flour, ginger, cloves and chili powder into the bowl. Using a wooden spoon, gradually combine the ingredients to make a stiff paste. Turn out onto a lightly floured work surface and knead lightly until smooth. Wrap and chill for 30 minutes.

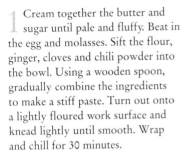

ICING GLAZE

This is like an ordinary cake glaze but is thinned with egg white so that it sets, making a thin, tangy cookie glaze.

*1 tablespoon beaten egg white
1 tablespoon lemon juice
½ cup confectioners' sugar*

♥ *Royal icing is ideal for piping decorations onto gingerbread.*

ROYAL ICING
The classic icing for gingerbread, this sets hard to give a good finish.

*1 egg white
1 cup confectioners' sugar*

1 Lightly beat the egg white. Beat in the confectioners' sugar, a little at a time, until the mixture is smooth and forms soft peaks. Transfer to a small bowl and cover the surface with plastic wrap, to prevent a crust from forming. Store in the fridge for up to three days.

1 Mix the egg white and lemon juice in a bowl. Gradually beat in the confectioners' sugar, until the mixture is smooth and has the consistency of light cream. The icing should thinly coat the back of a spoon.

KNEADING COLOR INTO SUGAR PASTE

You can buy colored sugar paste at supermarkets and suppliers of cake-decorating equipment, but you might find it more convenient to buy a pack of white sugar paste and color it as required. Paste food colors give the richest shades and are easy to use. Liquid colors can be used for pastel shades but they tend to make the paste quite soft.

1 Lightly knead the sugar paste on a surface dusted with confectioners' sugar, to soften it. Dot the icing with a little paste food coloring, using a toothpick. Knead in the color to the required shade, adding more color if necessary.

♥ COOK'S TIP ♥
If you don't want to use sugar paste right away, wrap it in plastic wrap and store it in a cool, dry place. Do not chill it or it will be difficult to work with.

USING TEMPLATES

A number of the projects require a template made from designs at the back of the book, or a shape cut from paper following the directions in the project itself. Trace the template onto waxed paper and cut it out. (You may prefer to copy the template onto thicker paper.)

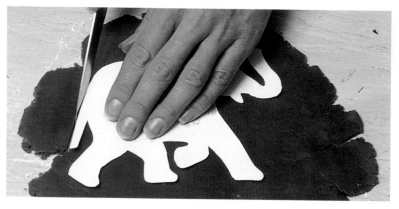

1 Roll out the gingerbread dough and lay the template over it. Carefully cut around the template and transfer the gingerbread dough to a cookie sheet.

TRIMMING COOKED GINGERBREAD

When you are going to assemble gingerbread into a cottage, castle or any other construction requiring straight edges, you will usually need to trim the edges straight again after baking, to ensure that the pieces will fit together. This is because the gingerbread will have spread and distorted slightly during the cooking process.

1 Once the gingerbread is cool enough to handle, lay it on a flat surface or board. Using a serrated knife, cut through the gingerbread with a gentle sawing action. It is a good idea to lightly hold the ginger-bread down with the hand not doing the cutting, to prevent it from moving around. If the gingerbread shape has been cut using a template, lay the template over the cooked gingerbread and cut carefully around it.

MAKING A PAPER PIPING BAG

1 Cut an 8-inch square of waxed paper in half diagonally so that you have two triangles. Hold one triangle with the longest side away from you. Curl the left-hand point over to meet the point nearest you, to make a cone. Curl the right-hand point over the cone.

2 Bring the points carefully together, to make a neat cone. Fold the points over several times, to secure the bag.

MELTING CHOCOLATE

1 Break the chocolate into pieces and put them in a small, heatproof bowl. Heat a small pan containing a little water to a very gentle simmer.

2 Place the bowl over the pan and let the chocolate melt. The base of the bowl should not touch the water or the chocolate will overheat. Stir gently and check that no lumps remain before using.

♥ *COOK'S TIP* ♥
One of the easiest ways to decorate gingerbread cookies is by using royal icing. Fill a paper piping bag with the royal icing, snip off the tip and drizzle on any design you choose.

♥ *Decorating cookies with white royal icing.*

CHOCOLATE FRUIT AND NUT COOKIES

These simple, chunky gingerbread cookies make a delicious gift, especially when presented in a decorative gift box. The combination of walnuts, almonds and cherries is very effective, but you can use any other mixture of candied fruits and nuts.

MAKES ABOUT 20
*1 quantity Lebkuchen mixture
8 ounces semisweet chocolate
¼ cup superfine sugar
⅓ cup water
¾ cup candied cherries
¼ cup walnut halves
1 cup whole blanched almonds*

1 Preheat the oven to 350°F. Grease two cookie sheets. Shape the dough into a roll, 8 inches long. Chill for 30 minutes. Cut into 20 slices and space them on the cookie sheets. Bake for 10 minutes. Leave on the cookie sheets for 5 minutes and then transfer to a wire rack and let cool.

2 Break the chocolate into pieces. Put the sugar in a small, heavy saucepan with the water. Heat gently until the sugar dissolves. Bring to a boil and boil for 1 minute, until slightly syrupy. Set aside for 3 minutes, to cool slightly, and then stir in the chocolate until it has melted and made a smooth sauce.

♥ *Carefully stack the cookies in a pretty box or tin, lined with tissue paper, or wrap in cellophane.*

3 Place the wire rack of cookies over a large tray or board. Spoon a little of the chocolate mixture over the cookies, spreading it to the edges with the back of the spoon.

4 Cut the candied cherries into wedges. Gently press a walnut half into the center of each cookie. Arrange pieces of candied cherry and almonds alternately around the nuts. Let set in a cool place.

♥ *COOK'S TIP* ♥
Store the cookies in an airtight tin until you are ready to eat them.

GINGERBREAD BOXES

*T*hese gingerbread boxes make lovely containers, for chocolates, candy or cookie gifts, and give you the opportunity to experiment with various decorative techniques, such as cutouts and

MAKES 1 LARGE AND 1 SMALL BOX
2 quantities Chocolate
Gingerbread
gold dusting powder
vegetable oil
4 ounces semisweet chocolate

♥ COOK'S TIP ♥
Once you have assembled both boxes, let them set, then line them with tissue paper and fill with chocolate, candy or cookies. Position the lids and wrap loosely with ribbons. Before allowing anyone to eat your boxes, remove the gold dusting powder decorations, as this powder is not edible.

1 Preheat the oven to 350°F. Roll out two-thirds of the dough and transfer to a greased cookie sheet. Cut out two 7 x 3½-inch rectangles for the base and lid of the larger box. Cut two 7 x 2¼-inch rectangles for the long sides and two 3½ x 2¼-inch rectangles for the short sides.

2 Using a decorative cutter, cut out a row of shapes from all the side sections. Roll out the remaining dough to make the smaller box. Make base and lid sections, 5 x 3 inches, the long sides, 5 x 2¼ inches and the short sides, 3 x 2¼ inches. Decorate the sides. Bake for 15 minutes. Cool, then trim.

3 Mix the gold dusting powder with a few drops of oil to a good consistency for painting. Paint a pattern around the cutout edges of the sides. Melt the chocolate. Put a little chocolate in a paper piping bag and snip off the tip.

4 To assemble the large box, pipe a little chocolate along the inside base edge of one side. Secure it to the base. Secure the remaining three sides, piping more chocolate down the corners. Assemble the smaller box in the same way.

WOODCUTTER'S COTTAGE

Unlike the other "buildings," this hut is assembled from "logs" of gingerbread dough to give it a rustic appearance. For presentation, light a couple of night-lights inside the hut, but don't leave them burning long, as the gingerbread will char.

2 quantities Chocolate Gingerbread
mixture
1 quantity Lebkuchen mixture
1 quantity royal Icing
10-inch square cake base
6 Tootsie Roll candies
confectioners' sugar, for dusting

1 Preheat the oven to 350°F. Line a cookie sheet with baking parchment. From paper, cut out a 6½ x 4-inch rectangle for the roof, two 6 x 3¼-inch rectangles for the hut front and back and two 3¼ x 2¼-inch rectangles for the hut sides.

2 Divide the chocolate dough into 14 pieces. Roll one piece under the palms of your hands into a rope 13½ inches long. Put it in the center of the cookie sheet. Repeat with the remaining small pieces of dough, spacing them on the cookie sheet about ⅛ inch apart. Bake for 15 minutes until the dough has risen. Let cool.

3 Lay the roof template over one end of the cooked gingerbread slab and cut it out. Cut out the sides, the front and back sections. Remove from the lining paper. From the front section, cut out a door and window.

4 Put some royal icing in a paper piping bag and snip off the tip. Using a palette knife, spread the cake base with the remaining royal icing. Pipe a little icing from the icing bag down the side of the front wall and secure to one side wall on the iced base. Secure the other side wall and back in the same way. Lay the roof section over the hut.

Make a template of the two trees (see back of book). Roll the Lebkuchen dough and cut out 10 large trees and 15 small trees. Bake on a greased cookie sheet for 10 minutes. Leave on the cookie sheet for 3 minutes, and then transfer to a wire rack.

5 Pipe a line of icing down one side of a tree section. Secure another straight side of a tree section against the first and place on the base. Add three more parts to make one tree. Construct and position the remaining trees in the same way.

6 Stack the Tootsie Rolls against one side of the hut as "logs." Place the roof section over the hut. To finish, dust the hut with confectioners' sugar.

♥ COOK'S TIP ♥
Before you begin cutting, lay all the template pieces on the gingerbread to find the most economical cutting layout.

GILDED GINGERBREAD CROWN

This project requires quite a bit of "propping up" and setting during the construction, but the results are impressive. Fill the crown with a selection of cookies or chocolates but don't pack them too tightly, or you may weaken it.

1 quantity Chocolate Gingerbread mixture
1 quantity Golden Gingerbread mixture
2 empty 14-ounce cans, washed
4 ounces semisweet chocolate
1 empty 1 pound, 12-ounce can, washed
2 ounces sugar paste
gold dusting powder
vegetable oil

1 Preheat the oven to 350°F. Roll out two-thirds of the chocolate mixture and cut out eight 4½ x 1¼-inch rectangles. Put on a greased cookie sheet. Roll out a little golden gingerbread mixture and cut out eight 1¼ x 1-inch rectangles. Cut a heart shape from each. Position these rectangles on the chocolate rectangles. Cut two strips of chocolate gingerbread.

2 From the strips, cut out eight triangles that measure 1½ inches along the short edge and 2 inches from the center of the short edge to the point. Cover the small cans with foil and support them on the cookie sheet. Lay three triangles over each can, so they bake in a curved shape. Bake the gingerbread, 5 minutes for the small pieces and 15 minutes for the large. Cool on a rack.

3 *(Left)* Melt the chocolate and let it cool slightly. Put in a paper piping bag and snip off a small tip. Wrap a band of waxed paper around the large can and stand it on a roll of tape or a can that will raise it by about 2 inches. Pipe a line of chocolate down one large rectangle and a dot of chocolate on the paper-covered can. Rest the rectangle against the dot of chocolate on the can. Pipe a line of chocolate around another rectangle and secure it to the first. Repeat all the way around, until the rectangles meet. (If they don't fit accurately, you might need to trim one rectangle slightly.) Set aside in a cool place to set. Remove the can and waxed paper and transfer the crown to a plate or board. Pipe little dots or scallops of chocolate down the seams in the gingerbread.

4 Pipe a line of chocolate along one rectangle top and secure a gingerbread triangle to it, propping the two up on a jar or carton until the chocolate has set. Repeat on the remaining sections; if necessary, set a few at a time. Roll the sugar paste into small balls and make a hole in each with a skewer. Pipe a dot of chocolate onto the tip of each triangle and gently press a sugar paste ball in position. Mix the gold dusting powder to a painting consistency with a few drops of the oil. Using the gold paint and a fine paintbrush, paint the balls and the edges of the hearts. Fill the crown with gingerbread cookies and arrange some others around the crown on the plate or board. Store in a cool place.

♥ *COOK'S TIP* ♥
The gold paint is for decoration only and should not be eaten.

DECORATED CHOCOLATE LEBKUCHEN

Wrapped in paper or cellophane, or beautifully boxed, these decorated cookies make a lovely present. Don't make them too far in advance, as the chocolate will gradually discolor.

MAKES ABOUT 40
1 quantity Lebkuchen mixture
4 ounces semisweet chocolate
4 ounces milk chocolate
4 ounces white chocolate
chocolate sprinkles
cocoa powder or confectioners' sugar, for dusting

♥ *COOK'S TIP* ♥

If the chocolate in the bowls starts to set before you have finished decorating, put the bowls back over the heat for a minute or two. If the chocolate in the piping bags starts to harden, microwave briefly or put in a clean bowl over a pan of simmering water.

1 Grease two cookie sheets. Roll out just over half the Lebkuchen mixture to 1¼ inches thick. Cut out heart shapes, using a 1¼ inch heart-shaped cutter. Transfer to the cookie sheets. Gather the trimmings with the remaining dough and cut into 20 pieces. Roll into balls and place on the cookie sheets. Flatten each one slightly. Chill both sheets for 30 minutes. Preheat the oven to 350°F. Bake for 8–10 minutes. Cool on a wire rack.

2 Break the semisweet chocolate into pieces and melt in a heatproof bowl over a small saucepan of gently simmering water. Melt the milk and white chocolate in separate bowls. Spoon a little of each chocolate into three paper piping bags and reserve. Spoon a little semisweet chocolate over a third of the cookies, spreading it slightly to cover them completely. (Tapping the rack gently will help the chocolate run down the sides.)

3 Snip just the very tip from the bag of white chocolate and drizzle it over some of the coated cookies.

4 Scatter the chocolate sprinkles over the semisweet chocolate cookies that haven't been decorated. Coat the remaining cookies with the milk and white chocolate and decorate some of these with more chocolate from the piping bags, contrasting the colors. Scatter more undecorated cookies with sprinkles. Let the cookies set.

5 Transfer the undecorated cookies to a plate or tray and dust with cocoa powder or confectioners' sugar.

CRENELATED CASTLE

This impressive castle would make a lovely birthday cake for any young child. If desired, you could add some chocolate soldiers or small, nonedible decorations. Bake the dough pieces in batches if necessary, and make sure that they are cooled on a flat surface.

1 quantity Lebkuchen mixture
2 quantities Golden Gingerbread mixture
7 ounces semisweet chocolate
4 ounces milk chocolate
14-inch square cake base or tray

1 Preheat the oven to 350°F. Grease two cookie sheets. Make one template (see back of book) of the castle back wall, one of the left side wall, three of the front, two of the keep ends, two of the front sides and one of the entrance. From paper, cut out two 5½ x 4½-inch rectangles for the castle keep sides, two 5 x 2½-inch rectangles for the roof and one 4½ x 2-inch rectangle for the drawbridge.

2 Roll out the Lebkuchen mixture to a 10½-inch square and transfer to a cookie sheet. Bake for 20 minutes, then cool. Roll out half the golden gingerbread. Lay some templates on the dough and cut around. Transfer to a cookie sheet. Roll out the remaining dough, and cut out the other shapes.

3 Bake the dough for approximately 15 minutes, until it begins to turn golden around the edges. Leave on the cookie sheets for 3 minutes and then transfer to a wire rack to cool. For the portcullis, draw two 2-inch squares on waxed paper. Melt the semisweet and milk chocolate in separate heatproof bowls over pans of barely simmering water. Put the melted chocolate in paper piping bags and snip off the ends. Pipe lines of the semisweet chocolate ⅛ inch apart on the squares. Pipe more lines in the opposite direction. Pipe four thick lines, 3½ inches long, onto the paper for the drawbridge "chains." Set aside in a cool place to set. (One trellis and two of the chocolate strips are "spares," in case of breakage!)

4 Pipe a line of melted semisweet chocolate around the entrance arch. Pipe another line about ½ inch from the crenelated top. Using the melted milk chocolate, pipe a decorative design around the arch. Pipe an outline around the top edge of the gingerbread.

♥ *COOK'S TIP* ♥
Let the chocolate cool slightly before using it to "glue" the castle sections together, otherwise the sections will not adhere. When securing the portcullis, use cool hands and work fairly quickly. Long, thin chocolate mints can be used instead of piped chocolate strips to create the drawbridge.

5 Pipe more semisweet and milk chocolate onto the other wall sections of the castle, lining up the walls so that the dark chocolate piping lines up. Let all the pieces set.

6 Carefully slide the Lebkuchen base onto a cake base or tray. Pipe a line of semisweet chocolate along the base of the entrance section. Place on the gingerbread base, about 2 inches from the front edge. Prop the section against a can for support.

7 Pipe more semisweet chocolate down one entrance side section and secure carefully in place, supporting as before. Secure the other entrance side section and then the front sections, in the same way. Strengthen by piping more chocolate down the seams and along the base on the inside. Let the chocolate set.

8 Carefully peel the paper from the piped chocolate square. Handling the chocolate as little as possible, pipe a little chocolate around the edges and then secure to the wrong side of the arch, to resemble a portcullis. Secure the remaining front section to the right side of the castle, at right angles to the front. Pipe a little chocolate along the exposed edge and then carefully rest one end section against it.

9 Pipe chocolate along the short sides of the side sections and stick them in place. Place the remaining wall sections of the castle in position, propping them up while they set, where necessary. Let the chocolate set. Secure the drawbridge in place with chocolate. Position the chocolate strips from the entrance walls to the drawbridge as the "chains," securing with a little chocolate.

10 Pipe more chocolate along the roof edges and then secure the roof pieces in position. Finally, use more chocolate to pipe small, cross-shaped windows over the castle walls. Let set in a cool place.

STEAM TRAIN

For presentation, set this magnificent train on a 13-inch square cake base that you have covered with a thin layer of gray or black sugar paste. Any gingerbread trimmings can be shaped into a simple track for the train.

3 quantities Chocolate Gingerbread mixture
2 empty 14-ounce cans, washed
6 ounces semisweet chocolate
6-inch-square chocolate sponge cake
confectioners' sugar, for dusting
¼ cup green sugar paste
¼ cup black sugar paste

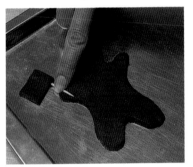

1 Preheat the oven to 350°F. Grease three large cookie sheets. From paper, cut out a 12 x 5-inch rectangle for the train base, a 5 x ½-inch rectangle for the bumper section, two 8 x 2-inch rectangles for the long sides and a 5 x 2¼-inch rectangle for the cab roof.

2 Roll out half the gingerbread dough on a floured surface and cut around the templates. Transfer to one cookie sheet. Cover each can with foil and support the cans on the second cookie sheet, wedging them with a little dough. Roll out more gingerbread and cut out two 4-inch squares. Lay the squares over the cans to shape them into curves. Make templates for the cab front and sides and the train front section, from the back of the book. Cut around the templates and transfer to the second cookie sheet.

3 Cut out a gingerbread man, using a 4-inch cutter, and transfer it to the third cookie sheet. Halve a toothpick and secure a small dough rectangle to one end for a flag. Lift one of the gingerbread man's arms and press the toothpick into it. Strengthen by gently pressing another gingerbread ball at the end of the arm.

♥ *COOK'S TIP* ♥
If you have any gingerbread mixture left over, reroll it and cut out another gingerbread man to serve as a stationmaster or guard. You could even make an extra batch of dough so that you can shape a selection of gingerbread "passengers." This is ideal for occupying younger members of the family while you get on with the more difficult modeling.

4 To make the wheels, cut out eight 1½-inch rounds, using a cookie cutter. Transfer to the third cookie sheet. Cut out the centers of the wheels using a slightly smaller cutter. Cut out two 1¼-inch wheels and remove the centers of these. Reroll the trimmings and cut out long, thin strips. Use to make the wheel spokes, cutting them to fit. Bake all the gingerbread, in batches if necessary, allowing 8–10 minutes for the wheels and 15 minutes for the larger sections. Leave on the cookie sheets for 3 minutes and then transfer to a wire rack to cool. (Stand the curved sections on one end to cool, so they don't collapse.) Trim the edges straight, if necessary.

▶

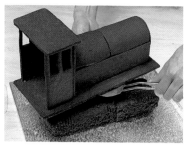

5 Melt half the chocolate and let it cool slightly. Put some in a paper piping bag and snip off the tip. Spread a little chocolate along one long side of a side section and secure this to the train base about ¼ inch in from the side and front of the train. Prop up the side with a jar until the chocolate has hardened. Position the other side section in the same way.

6 Spread more chocolate around the edges of the train front and stick it in position. Let set for 10 minutes. Spread melted chocolate around the edges of one curved section and gently rest it over the side sections. Position the second curved section. Use more chocolate to secure the train cab, first sticking the front in position, then the sides and finally the roof. Let set for 10 minutes.

7 Halve the sponge cake and lay the halves end to end on a board or tray to make a raised base, cutting off one end so that it is about 10 inches long. Using a spatula or palette knife, carefully lift the train and place it on the sponge cake. Use more chocolate to secure the bumper section to the front, propping it on a box or crumpled foil until set.

8 Thinly roll a little green sugar paste on a surface dusted with confectioners' sugar and cut out long, thin strips. Cut into short lengths and use to decorate the wheel spokes, securing with a dot of chocolate. Press a small ball of black sugar paste into the center of each. Secure the wheels to the sides of the cake with a little melted chocolate.

9 Melt the remaining chocolate and put it in a paper piping bag. Snip off a small tip. Use the chocolate to pipe little dots or scallops around the seams in the gingerbread. Pipe two additional rows of chocolate over the center of each curved section.

10 Thinly roll a little green sugar paste and cut into 1½-inch lengths. Secure in loops along the sides of the train. Use more green and black sugar paste to shape the remaining decorations, securing them with melted chocolate. Decorate the gingerbread man with sugar paste and secure him to the cab. Let set in a cool place.

GINGERBREAD TEDDY BEARS

These endearing teddy bears, dressed in striped pajamas, would make a perfect gift for friends of any age. If you can't get a large cutter, make smaller teddy bears or use a traditional gingerbread-man cutter. Just adding little semicircles of dough for ears instantly makes them teddy-bear-like!

MAKES 6
1 quantity Golden Gingerbread
mixture
3 ounces white chocolate
6 ounces white sugar paste
confectioners' sugar, for dusting
blue food coloring
1 ounce semisweet or milk chocolate

1 Preheat the oven to 350°F. Grease two large cookie sheets. Roll out the gingerbread dough on a floured surface and cut out gingerbread bears, using a 5-inch cookie cutter. Transfer to the cookie sheets and bake for 10–15 minutes, until they are just beginning to color around the edges. Leave on the cookie sheets for 3 minutes and then transfer to a wire rack to cool.

2 Melt half the white chocolate. Put it in a paper piping bag and snip off the tip. Make a neat template for the teddy bears' clothes: Draw an outline of the cutter on paper, finishing at the neck, halfway down the arms and around the legs. Thinly roll the sugar paste on a surface dusted with confectioners' sugar. Use the template to cut out the clothes, and secure them to the cookies with the chocolate. Use the sugar paste trimmings to add ears, eyes and snouts.

3 Dilute the blue coloring with a little water and use it to paint the striped pajamas, leaving a little white collar and painting in a waistline.

4 *(Left)* Gently melt the remaining white chocolate and the semisweet or milk chocolate in separate bowls over pans of barely simmering water. Put in separate paper piping bags and snip off the tips. Use the white chocolate to pipe a decorative outline around the pajamas and use the plain or milk chocolate to pipe the faces.

JEWELED ELEPHANTS

These elegant elephants make a lovely gift for animal lovers, or an edible decoration for a special occasion. If you make holes in them for hanging before baking, you could hang them as stunningly original Christmas tree decorations.

MAKES ABOUT 10
1 quantity Lebkuchen mixture
1 quantity Royal Icing
red food coloring
8 ounces sugar paste
small candy-covered chocolates
gold dragées

1 Preheat the oven to 350°F. Grease two large cookie sheets. Make a paper template for the elephant (see back of book). Roll out the Lebkuchen mixture. Use the template and a sharp knife to cut out elephant shapes. Space them slightly apart on the cookie sheets. Reroll the trimmings to make more elephants. Bake for about 12 minutes, until they are just turning golden around the edges. Leave on the cookie sheets for 3 minutes and then transfer to a wire rack to cool.

2 Put a little royal icing in a paper piping bag fitted with a small writing nozzle. (Alternatively, cut off the tip of the bag.) Knead some red food coloring into half the sugar paste. Roll a little red sugar paste under your fingers into fine ropes. Secure them around the feet and tips of the trunks, using icing from the bag. Shape more red sugar paste into flat oval shapes, about ¾ inch long, and stick them to the elephants' heads in the same way. Shape smaller ovals and secure them at the tops of the trunks.

3 Roll out the white sugar paste. Cut out circles, using a 2½-inch cookie cutter. Secure to the elephants' backs with royal icing so that the edge of the sugar paste is about 1 inch above the tops of the legs. Trim off the excess paste around the tops of the white sugar-paste shapes.

4 *(Left)* Pipe ½-inch tassels around the edges. Pipe dots of white icing at the tops of the trunks, around the necks and at the tops of the tails and also use it to draw small eyes. Halve the small candies and press the halves into the sugar paste, above the tassels. Decorate the headdresses, candy and white sugar paste with gold dragées, securing them with dots of icing. Set aside for several hours, to harden.

DOUBLE GINGERBREAD COOKIES

Packed in little bags or a gingerbread box, these pretty cookies would make a lovely gift.
They are easy to make, but will have everyone wondering how you did it!

MAKES ABOUT 25
1 quantity Chocolate Gingerbread mixture
1 quantity Golden Gingerbread mixture

1 Roll out half the chocolate dough on a floured surface to an 11 x 1¼-inch rectangle, ½ inch thick. Repeat with half the golden gingerbread dough. Using a knife, cut both lengths into seven long, thin strips. Lay the strips together, side by side, alternating the colors.

2 Roll out the remaining golden gingerbread dough with your hands to a long sausage, ¾ inch wide and the length of the strips. Lay the sausage of dough down the center of the striped dough. Carefully bring the striped dough up around the sausage and press it gently in position, to enclose the sausage completely. Roll the remaining chocolate dough to a thin rectangle measuring 11 x 5 inches.

3 Bring the chocolate dough up around the striped dough, to enclose it. Press gently into place. Wrap and chill for 30 minutes.

4 Preheat the oven to 350°F. Grease a large cookie sheet. Cut the gingerbread roll into thin slices and place them, slightly apart, on the prepared cookie sheet. Bake for 12–15 minutes, until just beginning to color around the edges. Leave on the cookie sheet for 3 minutes and then transfer to a wire rack to cool completely.

♥ *COOK'S TIP* ♥
For slicing the cookie dough before baking, use a knife that will cut through cleanly: A serrated kitchen knife usually works well. For a fresh supply of the cookies, bake them in batches; the shaped dough will store well in the fridge for up to a week; it also freezes well.

FRUIT-LADEN GINGERBREAD

*M*any *gingerbread recipes have a more spongy, cakelike texture than the gingerbread cookies used for constructions, and they can be flavored with dried fruits, nuts and a variety of delicious spices. This version contains plenty of raisins, ginger and orange and is decorated with candied fruits, perfect for a treat with fresh, strong coffee.*

SERVES 16
4½ cups all-purpose flour
1 teaspoon baking powder
1 tablespoon ground ginger
1 teaspoon ground cinnamon
2 cups raisins
⅞ cup blanched almonds,
roughly chopped
scant ¼ cup candied cherries, halved
finely grated rind of 1 orange
¼ cup chopped candied or
crystallized ginger
2 sticks sweet butter
1½ cups corn syrup
1 cup brown sugar
4 eggs, beaten
1 quantity Icing Glaze
1 pound mixed candied fruits

1 Preheat the oven to 375°F. Grease and line an 8-inch square cake pan. Sift the flour, baking powder, ginger and cinnamon into a bowl. Stir in the raisins, almonds, cherries, orange rind and half the candied or crystallized ginger. Heat the butter, syrup and sugar in a saucepan until the butter has melted. Add to the bowl with the eggs, and mix until evenly combined.

2 Transfer the gingerbread mixture to the pan and bake for 15 minutes. Reduce the oven temperature to 325°F and bake for another hour, or until the gingerbread is firm to the touch and a skewer, inserted into the center, comes out clean. Let cool in the pan.

3 Remove from the pan. Spread half the icing glaze over the top of the gingerbread and arrange the candied fruits and remaining candied or crystallized ginger over the glaze.

4 Drizzle the fruits with the rest of the glaze and let sit for several hours, until the glaze has set. Tie a ribbon around the cake, if desired, and serve cut in squares.

♥ COOK'S TIP ♥
This cake keeps well. Wrap and store in an airtight container before decorating it, adding the icing and fruits the day before you are going to serve it.

NOAH'S ARK

*T*his impressive creation is a lot of fun to make and would undoubtedly give great pleasure to a young child for a birthday celebration. Several animal templates are provided (see back of book) but you may already have plenty of animal cutters. If not, animal cutters are also widely available at kitchenware and gift stores.

3 quantities Golden Gingerbread mixture
scant ½ cup white chocolate
½ cup blue sugar paste
confectioners' sugar, for dusting
13-inch round silver cake base
¼ cup green sugar paste

1 Preheat the oven to 350°F. Line two large cookie sheets with waxed paper. Make templates of the ark sides, cabin ends and the animals, if using (see back of book). From paper, cut out a 10¾ x 3¼-inch rectangle for the deck, an 8¼ x 1½-inch rectangle for the ramp, two 5½ x 3¼-inch rectangles for the ark ends, two 4 x 1½-inch rectangles for the cabin sides and two 4½ x 2½-inch rectangles for the roof. Lay the ark sides template under the waxed paper on one cookie sheet.

2 Roll out half the gingerbread dough on a floured surface. Cut out long strips, ¼ inch wide. Lay one strip across the top of the template, so the edge of the dough is level with the edge of the template. Lay another strip so that it slightly overlaps the first. Repeat until the template is covered and then trim off the sloping ends. Slide the template from under the paper and make another side in the same way. Cut a 2-inch notch from the top edge of one side section, for supporting the ramp. Place the roof templates under the paper and lay strips on it in the same way. Roll out more dough and cut out all the remaining template shapes in the same way. Transfer to cookie sheets and bake, allowing about 10 minutes for the smaller shapes and 20–25 minutes for the ark sides. Leave on the cookie sheets for 3 minutes, then cool on a wire rack.

3 Melt half the chocolate in a bowl resting over a pan of barely boiling water and let it cool slightly. Put the chocolate in a paper piping bag and snip off the end. Pipe the melted chocolate down the long sides of one ark end and position it along the sloping side of one ark side. Prop them up with some sort of container so the side is supported at a 90° angle. Let set.

♥ *COOK'S TIP* ♥
For the best results, bake the gingerbread animals facing in the direction you want them to be on the finished cake (the underside will not be as smooth and attractive). Flip some of them over, still in pairs, before baking, if you want to have them facing different directions.

4 Secure the other ark end in place, supporting it as before. Gently rest the other ark side on the ends. Make sure the ark will sit squarely, once upright, by resting a flat tray against the ark base: All pieces should be level. Set the chocolate aside in a cool place to set.

5 Carefully turn the ark upright. Pipe more chocolate inside the ark, along the seams, to reinforce them. Set in a cool place to set. Assemble the cabin by piping chocolate down the sides of the pieces and sticking them together. Let set.

6 Pipe more chocolate along the edges of the roof sections and then carefully rest the roof in place. Pipe a little chocolate around the deck and lay it in position. Rest the cabin on top and let set in a cool place.

7 Thinly roll out the blue sugar paste on a surface dusted with confectioners' sugar. Lightly brush the cake base with water. Lift the sugar paste onto the base to cover two-thirds of it. Roll out the green sugar paste and use it to cover the remaining base so that it overlaps the blue sugar paste by about 1½ inch. Using a knife, cut a wavy line through the overlapping thicknesses of icing. Lift out the excess blue and green paste and smooth down the pastes so they meet in a neat, wavy line.

8 Carefully lift the ark onto the blue paste, toward the back of the base, so that when the ramp is positioned, it reaches the green paste. Melt the remaining white chocolate in a bowl resting over a pan of simmering water. Put the melted chocolate in a paper piping bag. Snip off a small tip. Use this melted chocolate to pipe little dots or decorative scallops around the seams of the ark. This acts as a decorative edging at the same time as giving additional strength to all the seams.

9 Use more melted chocolate to thinly pipe features onto the animals, that is, eyes, mouths, tails and so on. You can also try outlining other parts of their bodies to give the animals more definition. Stick the animals in pairs by sandwiching them, about ¼ inch apart, with a little left-over icing. Arrange the animals on the ark and the "land" in whatever way pleases you. The good thing about the freestanding pairs of animals is that you can arrange them until you are entirely happy with the results.

HANSEL AND GRETEL COTTAGE

*L*avishly decorated with an assortment of colorful candies, this gingerbread house is a lot of fun to
assemble. If you make it as a birthday cake, you will find that picking off the various candies is
much more exciting than eating a traditional sponge-based party cake.

2 quantities Golden Gingerbread
mixture
1 quantity Royal Icing
white chocolate buttons
colored hard candies
large selection of small candies
and gumdrops

♥ COOK'S TIP ♥
*The whole family can enjoy
decorating this cake, as "anything
goes!" It can also be reused
at Christmas with plenty of
candy canes and a light dusting
of confectioners' sugar.*

1 Preheat the oven to 350°F.
Grease two large cookie sheets.
From paper, cut out two 6¼ x 2¾-inch
rectangles for the cottage roof and
two 6 x 5½-inch rectangles for the
front and back. For the sides, cut
two 5½ x 3-inch rectangles, adding a
pointed roof section to one long side
that measures 1¼ inch from the tip of
the point to the edge of the rectangle.

3 Bake all the gingerbread, allowing
5 minutes for the small pieces
and about 15 minutes for the large
pieces, or until they just begin to
color around the edges. Leave on the
cookie sheets for 5 minutes and then
transfer to a wire rack to cool. Trim
the pieces, if necessary.

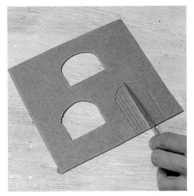

2 Roll out half the gingerbread.
Cut out twelve 2 x 1-inch
rectangles of gingerbread and cut
notches on one long side of each for
"curtains." Using the templates, cut
out the house sections. Cut out
windows from the front and side sections and mark a small door with a
knife. Mark vertical lines on the door
and cut out a small heart shape.
Reroll the gingerbread trimmings and
cut out a 9-inch round.

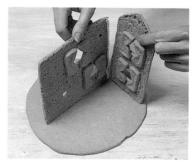

4 Put some royal icing in a paper piping bag and cut off the tip. Pipe a little icing down the long sides of the curtain sections and secure them to the insides of the windows, so the curtains show through.

5 Pipe a little royal icing down one short side of the front section and stick it at right angles to a side section, on the gingerbread base. Pipe more icing inside the house along the base, to hold it firmly. Use a can or jar to prop the walls in position while the icing sets (in a cool place).

6 Stick the other side section and back of the house in position. Pipe more icing along the top edges of the gingerbread and position the roof pieces. Let set in a cool place.

7 Pipe a wavy line of icing along the bottom edge of the roof and stick on a row of chocolate buttons. Pipe a line of icing above the buttons and stick on a row of hard candy. Repeat the layering to cover the roof.

8 Pipe another line of icing along the top of the roof and secure a row of halved chocolate buttons. Pipe dots of icing along the inner edges of the cottage curtains.

9 Use lots of candy and gumdrops to decorate the cottage, sticking pieces in place with plenty of royal icing. To make the front path, stick on pieces of broken chocolate buttons. Pipe simple flower outlines onto the walls and in the garden area and press small candies into the centers.

CANDY NECKLACES

These novelty necklaces are made from tiny gingerbread cookies, decorated and threaded onto ribbons. Arrange in a pretty, tissue-lined box or tin for presentation.

MAKES 12 NECKLACES
1 quantity Lebkuchen mixture
1 quantity Royal Icing
pink food coloring
selection of small candies
6 yards fine pink, blue or white
ribbon

♥ COOK'S TIP ♥
Use licorice whips instead of lengths of ribbon for threading the cookies to make totally edible necklaces, perfect for presenting as party favors.

3 Put half the royal icing in a paper piping bag and snip off a small tip. Use to pipe outlines around the star cookies. Color the remaining icing pale pink. Put it in a paper piping bag fitted with a star nozzle. Pipe stars onto the round cookies. Cut the candies into smaller pieces and use to decorate the cookies. Let harden.

1 Preheat the oven to 350°F. Grease two large cookie sheets. Roll out slightly more than half the Lebkuchen mixture on a lightly floured surface to a thickness of ¼ inch. Cut out stars using a 1-inch star cutter. Transfer the stars to a cookie sheet and spread them out evenly. Taking care not to distort the shape of the stars, make a large hole in the center of each one, using a metal or wooden skewer.

2 Gather the trimmings together with the remaining dough. Roll the dough under the palms of your hands to make a thick sausage about 1 inch in diameter. Cut into ½-inch slices. Put on the second cookie sheet. Using the skewer, make a hole in the center of each. Bake the gingerbread for about 8 minutes, until slightly risen and just beginning to color. Remove from the oven and, while still warm, remake the skewer holes, as the gingerbread will have spread slightly during baking. Transfer to a wire rack to cool.

4 *(Left)* Cut the ribbon into 20-inch lengths. Thread a selection of the cookies onto each ribbon.

MARQUETRY HEARTS

M arquetry is the decorative technique of inlaying contrasting-colored woods. Although very simple to do, fitting light and dark gingerbread shapes together to create a pattern or picture is very effective. Use this idea as inspiration for creating your own marquetry-style plaques.

1 quantity Chocolate Gingerbread
mixture
1 quantity Golden Gingerbread
mixture

1 Preheat the oven to 350°F.
Roll out the chocolate and golden gingerbread mixtures ¼ inch thick. Cut out twelve 1¼-inch squares from the chocolate gingerbread and thirteen 1¼-inch squares from the golden gingerbread. Assemble in a checkerboard design on a lined cookie sheet, with golden squares at the corners.

2 Using a 1½-inch heart-shaped cutter, neatly cut out a heart shape from each one of the golden gingerbread squares.

3 Using the same cutter, cut out 13 hearts from the remaining chocolate gingerbread and press them into the golden squares with heart-shaped holes. Using a ⅝-inch heart-shaped cutter, cut out heart shapes from the four chocolate hearts and position a golden gingerbread heart of the same size in the spaces.

4 (Left) Reroll all the gingerbread trimmings and cut four long, thin strips from each. Position a chocolate strip down each side of the cookie, overlapping them at the corners. Using a knife, miter the corners by cutting through both thicknesses and removing the dough ends. Position the strips of golden gingerbread mixture outside the chocolate border and trim the corners, as before. Bake for about 15 minutes. Let cool on the cookie sheet.

ROCKING–HORSE COOKIES

B rightly decorated with red and blue sugar paste, these simple rocking horses are really absorbing to make. Make them for gifts and pack them into pretty, tissue-lined boxes.

MAKES 6–8
1 quantity Lebkuchen mixture
1 quantity Royal Icing
⅛ cup red sugar paste
confectioners' sugar, for dusting
⅛ cup blue sugar paste
⅛ cup black sugar paste

♥ COOK'S TIP ♥
Reroll the gingerbread trimmings for the rockers. Cut straight strips and bend them gently into curves on the cookie sheets, making sure they are securely attached to the horses' hooves.

1 Preheat the oven to 350°F. Grease two large cookie sheets. Make a rocking-horse template (see back of book). Roll out the Lebkuchen mixture on a floured surface and cut out the shapes. Space them well apart on the cookie sheets. Cut out 6-inch-long strips, about ½ inch wide, to make the rockers. Bake the gingerbread for about 10 minutes, until slightly risen and just beginning to color. Leave on the sheets for 3 minutes and then transfer to a wire rack to cool.

2 Put a little royal icing in a paper piping bag fitted with a small writing nozzle. Roll out the red sugar paste on a surface dusted with confectioners' sugar. Cut out saddles, using the template as a guide, and stick one to each horse with a little royal icing. Thinly roll the blue sugar paste and cut it into long, thin strips. Secure these to the horses with a little icing, to form the reins and bridles.

3 Roll out the black sugar paste and cut out manes and tails, using the template. Stick them to the cookies in the same way.

4 Put more icing in the piping bag to pipe eyes and decorative designs on the saddles and rockers. Let set for several hours in a cool place.

GINGERBREAD STREET

Indulge your creativity with these pretty gingerbread houses, simply decorated with piped chocolate and hard candy "windows." Copy the design used here, or make your own street scene in the design and size of your choice.

MAKES 6–8
1 quantity Golden Gingerbread mixture
1 cup hard candy
2 ounces semisweet or milk chocolate
several thin sticks of chocolate

♥ *COOK'S TIP* ♥

If cutting out "door" sections, remember to leave a thin frame of gingerbread at the bottom, so that the candy doesn't run out as it melts, making an uneven edge.

1 Preheat the oven to 350°F. Line two cookie sheets with baking parchment. Draw a 6½ x 3¼-inch rectangle on a sheet of paper. Draw several roof outlines along one long edge and fill the rectangle with a variety of windows. Cut out the template.

2 Roll out the gingerbread dough on a floured surface, lay the template on top and cut around the template outline. Repeat the process for the other houses. Transfer to the cookie sheets and then remove the window sections. Bake for 5 minutes.

3 Lightly crush the hard candies by tapping them firmly, still in their wrappers, with the end of a rolling pin. Put the candy into the window areas of the gingerbread and bake for 5 minutes, until the candy melts to fill the windows. Cool on the cookie sheets.

4 Melt the chocolate and let it cool slightly. Put it into a paper piping bag and snip off the tip. Use the chocolate to pipe roof, window and door outlines on the cookies.

5 Pipe lines of chocolate under the windows and stick the chocolate sticks in place, cutting them to fit where necessary. Let sit in a cool place until the chocolate has set.

HARVEST PLAQUE

Decorated with simple fruits and flowers, this large cookie makes a delicious autumnal gift.
Loosely wrap it in tissue paper and pack it in a flat box or tin.

2 quantities Golden Gingerbread
mixture
⅛ cup white almond paste
several whole cloves, buds removed
½ quantity Royal Icing
orange, green and yellow food
coloring

1 Preheat the oven to 350°F.
Grease a cookie sheet. Roll out
two-thirds of the gingerbread dough
and cut out an 8½ x 7-inch rectangle.
Transfer to the prepared cookie
sheet. Using the handle end of a fine
paintbrush, make small, decorative
indentations around the edges. With
the tip of a knife, mark a line ⅝ inch
away from all the edges. Lightly
grease a sectioned mini-muffin pan.
Thinly roll the remaining dough and
cut out simple flower shapes, using
appropriate cutters.

2 Press the shapes against the sides
of the muffin pan so that they
bake in a cupped position. Roll small
balls from the trimmings and press
them into the centers. Reroll the
trimmings and cut out simple leaves,
each about 2 inches long and 1 inch
wide. Arrange the leaves in the pan
with the flowers, with some curving
into the muffin cups so they bake in
a curved shape. Bake the gingerbread
base for about 20 minutes and
the flowers and leaves for about
7 minutes. Let cool in the pan.

3 Lightly knead the almond paste
and divide it in half. Roll each half
into a ball and roll the balls over a
fine grater, to give a textured surface.
Slice them in half and press a clove
into each half to form the fruits.

4 (Left) Put a little of the icing in a
paper piping bag and snip off the
tip. Use to attach the flowers, fruits
and leaves to the gingerbread plaque.
(You might prefer to try a few different arrangements of decorations first,
before you stick them in place.) Dilute
the orange food coloring with a little
water and use it to paint the almond-
paste fruits, using a fine paintbrush.

5 Color half the remaining icing
green and thin it with a little
water, if necessary, to give a painting
consistency. Use to paint decorative
lines over the leaves. Color the
remaining icing yellow and use it
to paint the centers of the flowers
and a decorative line around the
edges of the plaque. Let set overnight
in a cool place.

FESTIVE WREATH

*U se this elaborate wreath as a table centerpiece over the festive season: The warm scent of ginger-
bread and spices will gradually fill the room. To bake the leaves in curved shapes, collect two or
three cardboard tubes from the centers of foil or wrapping paper and cover them with foil
before draping gingerbread leaves over them.*

2 quantities Chocolate Gingerbread
mixture
1 quantity Golden Gingerbread
mixture
8 cinnamon sticks
2 yards ribbon, about ¹/₂ inch wide
8–10 kumquats
cloves
⅛ cup red sugar paste
1 quantity Royal Icing
lemon juice
14-inch round gold cake base
(optional)

♥ COOK'S TIP ♥
*If you can find one, you could use a
large holly cutter for shaping the
leaves, although the points on
cutters are often quite rounded,
which doesn't look as effective.*

1 Preheat the oven to 350°F.
Grease two large cookie sheets.
Roll out two-thirds of the chocolate
gingerbread dough on a floured
surface until it is about 12 inches
in diameter. Transfer to one cookie
sheet. Using a large plate or bowl as a
guide, cut out a circle about 11 inches
in diameter. Cut a 7-inch circle out of
the center and lift out the dough, to
leave a ring of gingerbread.

2 Reroll the trimmings with the
remaining chocolate dough. Cut
out oval shapes, about 3¹/₄ inches long
and 2 inches wide. Using a small,
round cutter or the wide end of a
large piping nozzle, cut out flutes
from the edges of the oval, to shape
large holly leaves. Mark veins on the
leaves with a sharp knife.

▶

3 (*Left*) Put the foil-wrapped tubes on a cookie sheet, supporting them around the base with a little dough. Lay some leaves over the tubes. Make more leaves from the golden gingerbread, positioning some on the curved tubes and others flat on the cookie sheets. You will need about 40. Bake the gingerbread for 8–10 minutes, until the golden gingerbread is just starting to color around the edges. Leave on the cookie sheets for 3 minutes and then transfer to a wire rack to cool.

4 Tie pairs of cinnamon sticks with short lengths of ribbon. Stud the kumquats with plenty of cloves. Shape the red sugar paste into small "holly berries."

5 Put some royal icing in a paper piping bag and snip off the tip, so the icing can be piped in a thick line. Pipe a line of icing around a leaf. Using a paintbrush dipped in lemon juice, draw the icing from the center of the piped line toward the center of the leaf, to give a variegated look. Repeat on about a third of the leaves.

6 Carefully slide the gingerbread ring onto the cake base, if using. Pipe a dot of icing onto the tip of a leaf and stick it to the ring. Continue adding more leaves, gradually building up the design with the leaves arranged in different directions.

7 When the leaves are arranged, position the kumquats and cinnamon bundles, securing them with a little icing. Arrange the red berries in clusters among the leaves and finish with additional ribbon if desired.

GOLDEN CHRISTMAS TREE

*Y*ou can decorate this stunning tree with any combination of candy, chocolate and gingerbread
*shapes, provided they are not too heavy. It can be used for an impressive table centerpiece,
trimmed with plenty of gold or a brighter color scheme.*

*3 quantities Golden Gingerbread
mixture
1 quantity Royal Icing
gold dragées
11-inch round gold cake base
1 empty 14-ounce can, washed
selection of gold-wrapped candies
or chocolates
1¹/₂ yards fine gold beading
1¹/₂ yards fine gold ribbon*

1 Preheat the oven to 350°F.
Grease two large cookie sheets.
Thinly roll out just under half the
dough on a floured surface and
transfer to one cookie sheet. Cut out a
13 x 9-inch rectangle from the dough
on the cookie sheet; remove the
trimmings. Cut the rectangle
accurately in half lengthwise. Using
a long ruler or two pieces of paper
overlapping in a straight line as a
guide, cut diagonally from one corner
of a rectangle to the other. Repeat on
the second rectangle.

♥ *COOK'S TIP* ♥
*Make sure the gingerbread shapes
cool on a perfectly flat wire rack, as
they must be straight to allow you
to assemble the tree correctly.*

2 Roll just under half the remaining
dough, put it on the other cookie
sheet and cut it in the same way to
make four more triangles, as above.
Reroll all the trimmings with the
remaining dough and cut out a large
selection of stars, boots and other
suitable decorative shapes. (Make
some large stars, so you can stick one
to the top of the tree.) Using a knife,
cut out candy-cane shapes. Add to the
cookie sheets and cook, allowing
about 8 minutes for the small shapes
and 15–20 minutes for the triangles.

3 Immediately after the gingerbread
is removed from the oven, recut
the diagonal lines, as the mixture will
have risen slightly. Let sit on the
cookie sheets for 5 minutes and then
transfer to a wire rack to cool.

4 Trim the straight sides of the
triangles using a serrated knife.
Put a third of the icing in a piping bag
fitted with a writing nozzle. Pipe dots
of icing over one triangle and secure
gold dragées to the dots. Repeat on
the remaining triangles.

5 Put half the remaining icing in a
piping bag fitted with a star
nozzle. Pipe a line of icing down the
straight side of one triangle and along
the base. Repeat on another triangle. ▶

6 Secure the straight sides of the triangles together on the cake base, so they meet at right angles in the center of the base. Gently rest the empty can over the top of the triangles, to hold them together.

7 Gradually add the remaining triangles to the tree: First, position two so that there are four sections at right angles, each time carefully lifting off the can while positioning. Add the remaining four sections in the same way. Let set in a cool place for several hours. Lift away the can.

8 Use more icing in the star nozzle to pipe rows of stars over the seams between the tree sections. Decorate the un-iced sides of each section with more gold dragées, using tweezers if that makes it easier to reach the innermost areas.

9 Using the writing nozzle, decorate the little cookies, either by simply piping an icing outline or by adding additional features. Let set.

10 Stick the cookies to the tree by piping a little icing onto the edge of the gingerbread and then gently pressing them into place. Stick a large star to the top of the tree. Stick gold-wrapped candies between the cookies.

11 Put a dot of icing at the top of the tree behind the star, and secure the end of the gold beading. Loosely trail it around the tree, securing it in places with a dot of icing. Repeat with the ribbon. Let set.

STAINED-GLASS WINDOWS

These easy-to-make cookies look stunning displayed near a window or on the Christmas tree, where they will catch the glow of the Christmas lights.

MAKES ABOUT 10
1 quantity Golden or Chocolate
Gingerbread mixture
about 20 hard candies
fine ribbon or string

♥ COOK'S TIP ♥
These can be made 2–3 days in advance and wrapped between layers of plastic wrap. They can be hung for a few days, but after that the candy will begin to soften.

1 Preheat the oven to 350°F. Line a large cookie sheet with baking parchment. Make a window template (see back of book). Thinly roll out half the gingerbread mixture on a floured surface. Cut out windows using the template and transfer them to the cookie sheet. Reroll the trimmings with the remaining dough and make more windows. Use a metal skewer to make a hole in the top of each cookie. Bake the windows for 5 minutes.

2 Meanwhile, very lightly crush the hard candies by tapping them firmly, still in their wrappers, with the end of a rolling pin.

3 Remove the half-baked cookies from the oven and place a few pieces of crushed candy in each section of the windows. (You will need about two candies per window.) Return the cookies to the oven and bake for another 5 minutes, until the candies have melted to fill the windows. Remake the skewer holes, as the gingerbread will have spread a little during baking. Let the windows cool on the cookie sheet.

4 Thread a length of fine ribbon or string through the hole of each cookie, to hang them.

GLAZED GINGERBREAD COOKIES

The quantity you can make of these little cookies will depend on the size of the cutters you use. They also make good hanging cookies, for decorating trees and garlands. To hang them, make holes in the cookies with a skewer, and thread with fine ribbon.

MAKES ABOUT 20
1 quantity Golden Gingerbread mixture
2 quantities Icing Glaze
red and green food coloring
6 ounces white almond paste

1 Preheat the oven to 350°F. Grease a large cookie sheet. Roll out the gingerbread dough on a floured surface and, using a selection of cookie cutters, cut out a variety of shapes, such as trees, stars, crescents and bells. Transfer the cookies to the cookie sheet and bake for 8–10 minutes, until they are just beginning to color around the edges.

2 Leave on the cookie sheet for 2 minutes and then transfer to a wire rack and let cool. Place the wire rack over a large tray or plate. Using a small spoon, spoon the icing glaze over the cookies until they are completely covered. Let cool in a dry place for several hours.

3 Knead red food coloring into one half of the almond paste and green into the other half. Roll a thin length of each colored paste and then twist the two together into a rope. Secure a rope of paste around a cookie, moistening the icing with a little water, if necessary, to hold the paste in place. Repeat on about half the cookies.

4 Dilute a little of each food coloring with water. Using a fine paintbrush, paint festive decorations over the plain cookies. Let dry and then wrap in tissue paper.

CHRISTMAS TREE PLAQUES

*M*ake plenty of these pretty cookies and combine them with festive bows to hang on a tree that will then need little other decoration.

MAKES 12
1 quantity Golden Gingerbread
mixture
1 quantity Royal Icing
green and blue food coloring
lemon juice
silver dragées
fine ribbon

♥ *COOK'S TIP* ♥

You will need fine ribbon or string to thread these cookies. Alternatively, loop thicker ribbon through the spaces over the heads of the gingerbread figures.

1 Preheat the oven to 350°F. Grease two large cookie sheets. Roll out the gingerbread dough on a floured surface and cut out gingerbread figures, using a 3¼-inch cutter. Space them well apart on the cookie sheets.

2 Reroll the trimmings and cut them into strips, ½ inch wide and 11 inches long. Position a strip around one figure, so that the ends meet over the head and the curved edge just meets the limbs. Repeat with each of the remaining figures.

3 Use a skewer to make a hanging hole in the top of the outer frame. Bake the cookies for 12–15 minutes. Leave on the cookie sheets for 3 minutes and then transfer to a wire rack to cool.

4 Put a little of the royal icing in a paper piping bag fitted with a writing nozzle. Divide the remaining icing into two bowls. Color one half green and the other blue. Use a little lemon juice to thin the consistency of each, until the icing thinly coats the back of a spoon. Using the writing nozzle, pipe lines of white icing across the hands, feet and collars of the figures. Also, draw on a face.

5 Spoon a little colored icing onto the body, spreading it to the edges using a toothpick. Use the rest of the colored icing to coat the remainder. Secure a row of dragée "buttons," pushing them into a line with the tip of a skewer. Let set for about 2 hours. Decorate the edges of the cookies with white icing piping, securing dragées with dots of icing. Thread the cookies with ribbon for hanging.

CHRISTMAS COTTAGE

*T*his cottage is built using a very basic house shape, but the Christmas snow theme gives it a pretty, dreamy finish. The piped windows and doors should be left to harden for one or two days, so you might prefer to make them first.

2 quantities Golden Gingerbread mixture
1 quantity Royal Icing
11-inch round cake base
1½ pounds white sugar paste
confectioners' sugar, for dusting
2 tablespoons black sugar paste
2 tablespoons red sugar paste
2 tablespoons green sugar paste

1 Preheat the oven to 350°F. Grease two cookie sheets. From paper, cut out two 8 x 4¼-inch rectangles for the cottage roof. Cut two rectangles measuring 7½ x 3½ inch for the front and back. On the front, cut two 1¼ x ¾-inch windows and a small door. Cut two more windows on the back. For the sides, draw a 3½-inch square on paper and add a pointed gable onto one side, measuring 3 inches from the point to the base of the roof. Cut out two sides, adding a window in each.

2 Roll out the gingerbread dough on a floured surface and cut out all the templates. Transfer the gingerbread shapes to the cookie sheets and bake them for about 15 minutes, until they are just beginning to color around the edges. Leave on the cookie sheets for 3 minutes and then transfer to a wire rack to cool.

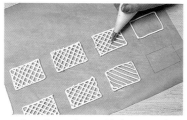

3 On a large sheet of baking parchment, draw seven 1½ x 1¼-inch rectangles. Mark one 2½ x 2-inch rectangle. Put a little of the royal icing into a paper piping bag fitted with a large writing nozzle. Pipe over the marked outlines on the paper. For the windows, pipe diagonal lines across the small rectangles and then across in the opposite direction. (One window is extra, in case of breakage!) Fill in the larger rectangle with lines of piping for the door. Let harden for 24–48 hours in a cool place.

4 Brush the cake base lightly with water. Roll out 8 ounces of the white sugar paste on a surface dusted with confectioners' sugar and use it to cover the base, trimming off the excess around the edges. Put more royal icing in a paper piping bag and cut off the tip. Pipe a line of icing down one short side of the cottage and stick it at right angles to a side section on the base.

5 Pipe more icing along the base on the inside. Secure the back and remaining side sections in the same way. Peel the lining paper away from the windows. Pipe a little icing around the edges of the windows and stick them in place. Secure the door in the same way. Let harden for 1–2 hours in a cool place.

6 Pipe more icing over the top edges of the cottage and secure the roof sections. Spread a little icing over the roof area. Roll out another 12 ounces of the white sugar paste to an 8-inch square. Lift it over the roof, so that it covers the gingerbread. Neaten the edges of the sugar paste.

7 Using a thin nozzle, drizzle bits of icing down from the roof to look like icicles. Use the black sugar paste to shape small window sills and a doorknob. Secure with a little icing. Lightly knead a dot of the black sugar paste with a little of the white until marbled. Break off small pieces and flatten them into "stones" for the path. From the remaining white sugar paste, shape small cones for trees and secure with a moistened paintbrush. Roll a little red and green sugar paste as thinly as possible. Twist into ropes and use to decorate the front door and some of the trees. Lightly dust the cottage with confectioners' sugar.

♥ *COOK'S TIP* ♥
Once the sugar paste is in place on the cottage roof, you may find it easier to trim the edges with a pair of sharp scissors than with a knife. Mold the paste over the edges of the gingerbread to look like thick snow.

TEMPLATES

CRENELATED CASTLE
(KEEP ENDS)

CRENELATED CASTLE
(ENTRANCE)

JEWELED ELEPHANTS

CRENELATED CASTLE (LEFT SIDE)

STAINED-GLASS WINDOWS

CRENELATED CASTLE
(BACK)

CRENELATED CASTLE
(FRONT)

CRENELATED CASTLE
(FRONT SIDES)

WOODCUTTER'S COTTA

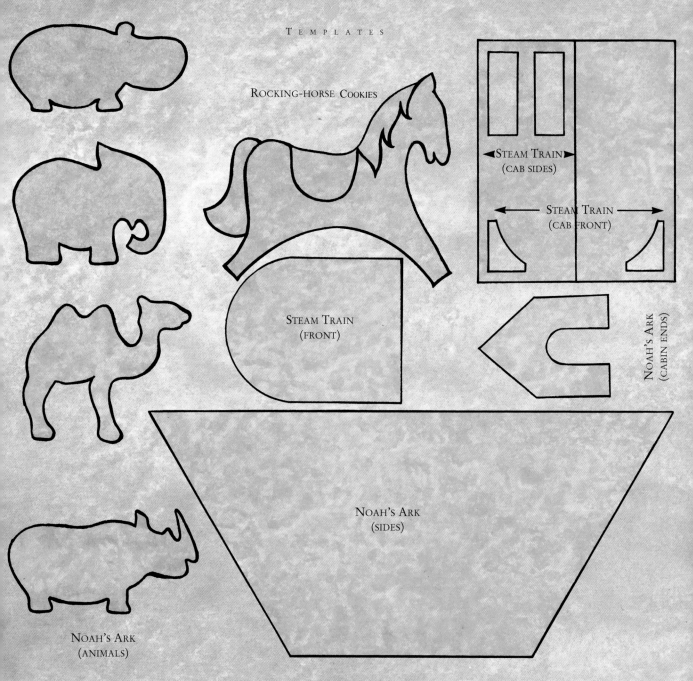

ROCKING-HORSE COOKIES

STEAM TRAIN
(CAB SIDES)

◄STEAM TRAIN►
(CAB SIDES)

STEAM TRAIN
(CAB FRONT)

STEAM TRAIN
(FRONT)

NOAH'S ARK
(CABIN ENDS)

NOAH'S ARK
(SIDES)

NOAH'S ARK
(ANIMALS)

INDEX